Intimacy the Beginning of Authority

By Catrina J. Sparkman

Intimacy the Beginning of Authority
Copyright © 2013 Catrina J. Sparkman
Published by The Ironer's Press
SOFTCOVER EDITION
ISBN 13: 978-1-949958-13-3

All rights reserved. No part of this book may be reproduced, stored in whole or in part or transmitted in any form by any means, without prior written permission from the publisher, except in the case of brief quotations embodied in articles for review. Nor can this book be circulated in any form of binding or cover other than that in which it is published.

All Bible Scriptures taken from the following translations: New International Standard Version, God's Word Translation, English Standard Version, and or The King James Version.

DEDICATION

To all the faithful warriors across the earth, hidden men, women, and children, God has mobilized for such a time as this.

TABLE OF CONTENTS

Author's Note

Chapter 1
The Nature of God-1

Chapter 2
My Testimony-14

Chapter 3
God is Relational-37

Chapter 4
God is Generational-54

Chapter 5
He Honors His Word Above All Else-73

Chapter 6
God is Territorial-89

Chapter 7
Intimacy the Beginning of Authority -111

Epilogue
An Invitation -115

About the Author-117

AUTHOR'S NOTE

Dear Reader,

I want to take a moment to thank you for purchasing your copy of this book. In a world where your attention can be pulled in so many other directions, thank you for having a heart to go deeper in the things of God.

My prayer is that this book will bless you, that as you read it, you will receive an impartation from on high that will transform your outlook on heaven and your relationship with the Living God forever. I'm also asking the Father to teach you *how* to enjoy the road. As humans we are often consumed with the idea of getting from where we are right now, to this majestic and oftentimes elusive place called 'there'. However, I've learned that in God's way of thinking, the path or road you travel is just as important as the destination spot.

Now there's no doubt about it, God wants us to get to the finish line and He wants us to finish strong. He also wants for us to delight ourselves in the journey. Transformation doesn't occur when we get 'there'. Transformation happens along the way. Transformation happens when God, the Word made Flesh, begins to teach us, and talk to us while we are sitting in our houses, while we are walking along the path, when we lie down and when we rise up. (Deuteronomy 11:19). An eternal friendship will be forged between yourself and the Creator of the Universe when you meet Him in the road. Thank you for participating in this journey. Thank you for sowing into fertile ground—both yours and mine. Welcome to *Intimacy the Beginning of Authority*.

In His service,

Catrina J. Sparkman

HOW TO USE THIS BOOK

If you take a moment and quickly flip through the pages you will find the following divisions: **Chapters, Selah Notes,** and **Discussion Questions.**

SELAH NOTES

The word Selah is used 74 times in the Bible. Whenever you see the word Selah it simply means to pause and think about what you have just read. I've placed Selah Notes throughout this book to aid in your prayer and reflection time. Use the Selah Notes to jot down impressions about what you've just read, prayers or declaration, as well as any thoughts or stirrings that the Holy Spirit brings to your mind.

DISCUSSION QUESTIONS

This book is designed to be a six week study course in intimacy. There are a total of forty-two discussion questions, seven at the end of each chapter. The questions are broken up in this way so that you can easily study one chapter a week, and reflect on one question a day.

However, please be aware that this is only a suggestion. Everyone's learning style is different, so feel free to complete the study portion of this book in any manner that works for you. If you have purchased this book as part of a seminar or class please see the discussion leader for instruction per the appropriate break down of the study portion of the class.

CHAPTER ONE

THE NATURE OF GOD

> When you read the Old Testament, you begin to understand what causes God's anger to burn. What makes Him jealous and what makes Him laugh. The Old Testament will show you God's nature.

I have been on a lifelong quest to discover the nature of God. You see I have a theory, and my theory is this: I believe that if you understand God's nature you will be less likely to offend Him. Much of what I have learned about the nature of God comes from studying the Bible, particularly the Old Testament. Now of course, I realize that there are some people in Christendom today who believe that there is little value in reading the Old Testament. After all, the Old Testament is the Book of the Law, and Christians today are no longer under the law. We are partakers of a new covenant—a covenant of mercy and grace. Furthermore, these people say that if the Old Testament was so valuable then why is it that the majority of street preachers only hand out New Testament Bibles to would-be-converts? Isn't the centrality of the Christian faith Jesus and the message of the Gospels? Well the answer to that question is an unequivocal yes.

Still, you can call me old fashioned, but I'm an Ezekiel 3:3, and a Revelation 10:10 type of girl. I believe in eating the whole scroll. I believe that you can't even begin to fully understand the incarnate Christ without reading the Old Testament. I believe that when you eat the whole Word of God, you have the advantage of seeing the Living God, who is outside of time, through the lens of time. It just helps our puny minds to understand Him better. And truly, what Jesus said about the law, in reference to Himself is true, "It testifies of me," (John 5:39). The Old Testament will show you God's heart towards humanity. As you read the Scriptures you will meet a patient and long-suffering King. You will begin to catch but a mere glimpse of how long He has strived with wayward mankind. You will begin to see what causes His anger to burn. What makes Him jealous and what causes the God of Glory to laugh. You do know that, don't you? God laughs. The Old Testament will show you His nature. On this road to discovery I've learned four things about God's nature that I'd like to share with you in this book. This is by no means an all-inclusive list.

> ✝
>
> **Understanding these concepts will change how you approach the heavenly realms. Once this happens, it will inevitably shift the outcome of your prayers.**

There are many facets to our wonderful God, and it would take an eternity to just begin to tap the surface of who He really is. But I do believe that if you would understand these four aspects—and by understand I mean to figuratively and spiritually stand under these concepts, allow them time, room, and space to saturate your mind and heart—they will change how you approach the heavenly realms. And once your mind is changed, it will inevitably shift the outcome of your prayers.

I believe that, as they have done for me, these four concepts will help you to understand our God better. They will help you to see what He requires of you and also what He desires for your life. They will lead you into a place of intimacy with Him, and intimacy, my friends, is truly the beginning of authority.

The four points I want to make about our God are listed in bold lettering below. Take a moment to get to know them, commit them to memory, and wrap your mind around their meaning, as they will become the focal point of our study in the upcoming chapters.

1. **GOD IS RELATIONAL**

2. **GOD IS GENERATIONAL**

3. **GOD HONORS HIS WORD ABOVE ALL ELSE**

4. **GOD IS TERRITORIAL**

SELAH NOTES

CHAPTER 1
DISCUSSION QUESTIONS:

In chapter one, we discussed the value of reading the Old Testament to help us understand the personality of God. Read the story of King Hezekiah's life outlined in: 2 Chronicles, chapters 29-32; 2 Kings, chapters 18-20; and Isaiah, chapters 38-39. Answer the following questions:

1. Which of the four principles given at the end of Chapter 1 are present and at work in the above passages? What do these chapters tell you about God's nature?

_____
_____
_____
_____
_____
_____
_____
_____
_____
_____
_____
_____
_____

2. What human-like traits, if any, do you see in God the Father as you read these chapters?

3. King Hezekiah cries out to God, and God changes his mind concerning his future. Why do you think God had decided the king should die in the first place?

4. Why do you think God changed His mind about King Hezekiah?

_____
_____
_____
_____
_____
_____
_____
_____
_____
_____
_____
_____
_____
_____
_____
_____
_____
_____
_____
_____

5. Considering the events of Isaiah chapter 39, and also what the writer says in 2 Chronicles 31 and 32:24-25, tell whether or not you think it would have been better for Hezekiah to die.

6. Is it possible for the Lord to give us something that is not in our best interest? Read Numbers 11. Explain why or why not.

7. At times during Hezekiah's life, he seems to express doubt as to whether or not God really hears him. However, 2 Kings 20 tells us that Isaiah hadn't made it out of the courtyard when the Word of the Lord came to him with the answer to Hezekiah's request. What does this story teach you about heaven, God's ability to hear, and intercession?

_____
_____
_____
_____
_____
_____
_____
_____
_____
_____
_____
_____
_____
_____
_____
_____
_____

CHAPTER TWO

MY **TESTIMONY**

I want to start off this chapter by doing something that I rarely do, and that's give my personal testimony. You might be saying to yourself right about now, "What committed Christian doesn't give their testimony every chance they get?" Well, if you aren't saying it the diehard evangelists reading this certainly are.

In all fairness, I must say, that I've heard some amazing testimonies. I've heard stories of Jesus bringing folks back from the dead, healing people from sexual brokenness—most everyone in the church world by now has heard of Juanita Bynum's personal testimony entitled, *No More Sheets*. I've heard testimonies of people being struck by lightning and of crack house conversions.

Even the apostle Paul talks about the many troubles and perils he faced for the sake of the gospel. Countless times he was put in prison, five times he was beaten with the lash, three times with rods, once he was stoned, (I didn't even know a person could survive a stoning until I read Paul's testimony). Paul said three times he was shipwrecked, left floating on the open sea for a whole night and a day (2 Corinthians 11:23-28). So, I must warn you, before I begin, that my testimony is nothing like that at all. That's why I don't tell it often—because it's just not gritty enough. In fact, if the Hollywood motion picture industry were to rate my story, it would be rated G, not even PG. Nevertheless, it's my story, it's the path that the Lord took me on, and it's the story that has quintessentially made me, me.

I came to the Lord when I was fifteen. I accepted the gift of salvation, and Jesus became my Savior. Now mind you, I said He became my Savior. He had not yet become my Master or my Lord. That is to say that I did not live my life in such a way that I attempted to obey God's every command. I had received the precious yet free gift of salvation. This gift qualified me to join the family of God, but it alone did not grant me access to all the other rooms in the Father's house. As a newly saved convert to the kingdom, I was a friendly acquaintance of Jesus, standing inside the door of His home. I was inside the foyer. You may remember that in John 14:2, Jesus told his disciples, **"In my father's house there are many mansions. I go ahead of you to prepare a place."** Most times when we hear these words we think that Jesus is simply talking about preparing a place for us in the afterlife. But how many of us know that there is nothing simple about Jesus? Many times when He spoke, Jesus spoke to His followers in riddles and parables. So we can trust that there was always something else, a deeper meaning behind every word Jesus ever spoke—a subtext behind the text. I believe that when Jesus spoke these words to His disciples, He wasn't merely talking about a dwelling place in the hereafter. He was speaking about a "right now." I believe that when Jesus said, "I go to prepare a place for you," what He was saying was "Salvation is just the foyer. There are many levels and dimensions in me." Becoming a child of God is only the beginning. After you become a believer, you are entitled to and should expect to see and be invited into so much more.

> ✝
>
> **In my Father's house there are many mansions. Salvation is just the foyer. I want to be invited into more.**

But like everything of value, there are certain conditions or criteria that must be met before we can experience the "more" of God. For starters, we have to move past the point of merely being acquainted with Him and enter into a real loving relationship with Him. Through this relationship we gain access to all the other marvelous rooms in the Father's house. My heartfelt prayer for the new believers, who are reading this, is that a holy hunger will be awakened inside of you. May you never be content to stop at salvation. May a hunger and thirst for righteousness spring up on the inside of you that propels you past the foyer of God's love into the vast treasury of His riches.

As you participate in this study, I want you to keep these words of Jesus in the forefront of your mind: In my Father's House there are many mansions. Repeat the following declaration to yourself daily, as you complete this six-week study:

In My Father's House There Are Many Mansions, Salvation is Just the Foyer, I want more.

Let this become your mantra. I invite you to tug on heaven daily with these words until they become a living truth in your soul, until you find yourself soaring from level to level and dimension to dimension in Him.

My Testimony-The Break Up

I came to Christ when I was fifteen. But on my sixteenth birthday everything changed. My sixteenth birthday turned out to be the worst day of my old life and the first day of my new life. I had a boyfriend, my first boyfriend—who by the way, was not saved. Now, for the sake of full disclosure, shortly after I had given my life to Christ, I had been feeling the nudging of the Holy Spirit, telling me to break up with this boy because he was not equally yoked with me. My response to the Holy Spirit was, "No way, Holy Ghost, do you see how cute he is? And he likes me."

> **Oftentimes during their developmental stages, God will hide His prophets.**

"Besides," I told the Lord, "I have a plan. I will minister to him and bring him into the kingdom."

Reader, I beseech you in love, if you have not yet given missionary dating a try, DON'T, because it doesn't work. This boy breaks up with me on my sweet sixteenth birthday. *Ouch!* He doesn't have the decency to tell me it's over. He is just publicly seen with somebody else. Now all my friends feel it's their personal duty to inform me that I have officially been dumped. Remember, this is high school, so reputation is everything. My rep is on the line, so now, I feel as though I have no other choice, really, but to lie. So I boast, and I blustered to all of my friends about what an idiot this boy was, how I had already broken up with him on the telephone the night before. But inside I was crushed, I was heartbroken. I couldn't wait to get home, crawl into the bed and cry.

Now, for someone else this may not have been a big deal at all, but for me, it was tragic. Partly because I was sixteen and everything is tragic when you are sixteen. But also partly because of my divine spiritual make-up. I was somewhat of a wallflower in high school. I felt invisible. The truth of the matter is that there was a prophetic call on my life even then. God didn't want that call compromised so He hid me. I have found that often during their developmental stages, God will hide His prophets.

In fact, if you really study the prophets of the Bible, you will find that for majority of the prophetic people operating, the Bible never even tells you their names. You only know the handful of prophets that God puts on center stage.

> ✝
>
> **Leaders, even when prophetic people are off track they need to be handled carefully. When you have a wounded prophet in your mist the gifts won't flow purely or correctly.**

Now the statement could be made that we only know the names of the few, because there just weren't that many prophets around back then. You wouldn't be alone in your assessment if you believe that. The prophet Elijah certainly believed it. After his showdown on Mount Carmel with the false prophets of Baal, he ran and hid from Jezebel in a cave. Elijah cried out to God saying, "Lord, this woman has killed all your prophets and I am the only one left!" Remember what God told Him? "You aren't the only one. I have seven thousand who have not bowed down, nor kissed Baal's hand," (1 Kings 19). Isn't that beautiful? Ahab, Jezebel's husband, was the most terrible king in all of Israel's history. The times and seasons were so completely turned over to pagan worship and yet God had seven thousand prophetic voices in that land who were hidden from plain view.

Why does God hide the prophets? I think it is because of the covenant of friendship that He has with the prophets. The prophet is the only office listed in the five-fold ministry that God refers to as His friend. "I'll do nothing in the earth," He says, "unless I first reveal it to my servant the prophet," (Amos 3:7). Prophets are very sensitive people. Some might say they are overly sensitive. They have to be in order to hear in both this realm and the next. However, along with an increased sensitivity comes the ability to be easily wounded. That's why I think God hides these vessels. This is also why, leaders, even when prophetic people are off track, they need to be handled carefully because they can be easily wounded. Firstly, it's the law of love, and secondly for a very practical reason, when you have a wounded prophet in your mist, the gifts won't flow purely or correctly, and then you've got an even bigger problem on your hands.

As I said, I was a wallflower in high school, but for some reason this boy saw me. Now, the extent of our relationship was walking to class together, talking on the phone at night, and holding hands in the hallways at school. And I was thoroughly convinced that I was in love. The walking to class together, holding hands, that was enough for me, although most of my contemporaries at this point were doing so much more. The irony of this is that I grew up in Milwaukee, Wisconsin. By the mid to late 80's Milwaukee had the highest teen pregnancy rate in the nation.

> ✝
> **If you ever really want to know what is in your heart, listen to what comes out of your mouth. Out of the mouth the heart truly does speak.**

I was what you'd call a late bloomer. A voracious reader, I grew up on a lot of Sweet Dreams Romance novels. On the last page the boy got the girl. That's it. The end of the book—the grand finale was a kiss. This boy was firmly rooted in my mind as the love of my life and we had never even kissed. Needless to say, I turned out to be too slow for him. So he got in the fast lane.

So I get home, it's my sixteenth birthday, and I fully intend to have it out with God, who of course, I held responsible for allowing this horrible thing to happen to me, on—of all days—my sweet sixteenth birthday. I went upstairs to my bedroom. I grabbed a notebook and a pen and I began to write. Now remember, I'm supposed to be really upset about my break up, but listen to what I tell the Lord. Never once do I even mention this boy's name. If you ever want to know what's really in your heart, listen to what you say. Because out of the mouth the heart truly does speak.

So, this is what I said to God: "God, you talk to everybody but me. You talk to my mama. You talk to my daddy. You talk to my pastor. You talk to everybody up at the church, but not me. If you love me so much, why don't you talk to me? Well, you know what I'm going to do? I'm going to sit here tonight until you speak to me. I don't care if it takes all night long. I'm going to sit here until you speak to me." Now let me paint the picture for you. I'm upstairs in my bedroom, on the floor with my four in one color pen in hand and my favorite spiral bound pink paper notebook. I'm crying my eyes out as I write because my heart is broken. I'm feeling majorly rejected. Every false confidence I'd ever created for myself has, suddenly, in the last eight hours, been blown out of the water—when the most amazing thing that can ever happen to anindividual happens to me. God speaks.

> ✝
>
> **Today I bring you out from Egypt. My joy replaces your pain and a healing process can now begin.**

HE SPEAKS

It didn't take an hour, or all night as I had supposed it would. I heard the still small voice of God, speaking on the inside of me. I heard Him clearly, and immediately. He said, "You have no

> **✝**
>
> **Pay attention whenever God says something more than once. It means He knows you don't believe it and He wants you to stand up under it.**

idea how long I've been waiting for this. I've been with you all along, and I've been waiting for this." Then He spoke the words that would forever change the course of my life. He said, "Today, I bring you out from Egypt. My joy replaces your pain and a healing process can now begin." The thrill of that moment—when heaven first touched earth for me, and I heard my Creator's voice—has been the single most defining moment of my life. In an instant, all the pain left my heart. Remember, I told you prophetic people are really sensitive, so when that boy broke up with me, I felt a physical, crushing pain in my heart. I met the Lover of my soul on September 12, 1989, and He became my best friend.

The Triune God became everything to me. I always wanted a big brother, so Jesus became a big brother to me. I didn't have the best relationship with my earthly father at the time; my concept of a father figure was really screwed up, so Abba, the Father became Daddy God, to me. The Holy Spirit became my ultimate counselor, coach, teacher, and friend. Every day of my being and becoming life, I could see Jesus in my mind's eye, pull me onto His lap and tell me, "I AM yours and you are mine." Every day He told me this, until I believed it. Even now, to this day, when I hear Him say it, my stomach still turns flips.

Pay attention to whenever God says anything more than once, whether it is to you personally, or in His Word. When the God of Glory repeats Himself, it means He really means it. Actually, let me say it like this. He's not like man, so He never lies. You can trust that He means everything that He says, but when He says something more than once it's because He knows you don't believe it, and He really wants you to stand under it.

A few years later when I was in college I dated another guy for a second. I mean a really, really, hot second. We hadn't been talking for more than a week, when one day he tells me: "I'm sorry, I really like you, but I can't see you anymore. There's just something about you. It's like you have a force field around you. I can't really explain it, but it's like you already have a boyfriend. I feel like if I ever touch you, something bad will happen to me." By this time, I was fully secure in the Father's love, so there was no heartache whatsoever. I just said, "Okay, see you around."

But then it occurred to me to ask the question, "Holy Spirit are you blocking these men from me?"

> ✝
>
> **The Spirit of the Wrong Man —male or female— will take you off course and change the trajectory of your life.**

"I AM yours and you are mine," the Spirit said to me quietly. When God tells you something more than once, believe it. It wasn't until years later when I entered into the ministry of healing and deliverance that I would understand that one of the major spirits that the Lord was protecting me from was the Spirit of the Wrong Man. The Spirit of the Wrong Man (male or female) will take you off course and change the trajectory of your life. I talk more about the Spirit of the Wrong Man in my book, ***The Dishwasher Anointing.***

Today I can honestly say that every year since my sixteenth birthday, the Lord has given me some of the most remarkable gifts, always on or around my birthday. Just two years later in 1991 I arrived at the University of Wisconsin Madison. There I met Wesley Sparkman, the right man, September of my freshmen year. We had four classes together on a college campus of over 41,000 students, and of that number even a smaller percentage of those students were African American—which we both happen to be. We became best friends. That is to say Wesley became my best friend on the planet. Six years later, on my birthday, September 12, 1997, he asked for my hand in marriage and I accepted.

Now, I'm a romantic at heart. As I said before, I grew up reading all those Sweet Dreams Romance novels. So the early days with the Lord were times of beauty and wonder. God would say the most lovely things to me. As a child I never smiled. I come from a family that loves to take pictures, and I would get fussed at for not smiling in school pictures. My mother would say, "Catrina, I paid all this money for these school pictures, why won't you smile?" I couldn't really tell her why. I wasn't a particularly unhappy child. I just didn't smile. It just wasn't something I did. One day the Lord and I had the following conversation:

> **HIM**: Do I make you happy?
> **Me**: Yes, Lord, you know that you do. I've never been this happy in my entire life.
> **HIM**: I want the joy inside of you to shine forth for the world to see. And I want to teach you something in the process.
> **Me**: What's that?
> **HIM**: I want you to see that My Presence on the inside of you is so great it can change the world. So I will make a deal with you. Every time you smile, I will bring the sun out.
> **Me**: (*doubtful*) Uh . . . Really? I mean what if it's like raining?

HIM: I don't care what the weather looks like. If you smile, I'll bring out the sun out.

I didn't understand it at the time but this was my Karate Kid training time. Remember the movie the *Karate Kid*, not the remake, but the original 1984 version? Ralph Macchio's character, Daniel Larusso, thinks he's going over to Mr. Miyagi's house, played by Pat Morita, to learn some karate. Mr. Miyagi immediately puts him to work waxing cars and painting fences. This goes on for days until one day Daniel totally snaps.

He tells Mr. Miyagi, "I came to you to learn karate and you've turned me into your personal slave!"

Mr. Miyagi gets Daniel's attention by shouting one word at him, "Fight!"

It is in this moment that Daniel realizes the two basic arm movements he had practiced over and over again, while painting the fence, and waxing the car, would be the foundational moves in his karate skill arsenal.

Sure enough, no matter what the weather looked like, whenever I would smile, God kept His Word to me and brought the sun out. And boy did I test that one out time and time again. This was my training time, and I didn't even know it. He was teaching me countless foundational truths that would forever more be a part of my spiritual arsenal. Listed below is a quick list of some of the things I learned from this experience about both Him and me.

What I learned about Him

1. Miracles are small potatoes to God.
2. God is trustworthy, He always keeps His Word.
3. **Everything, including the sun, works for God.**

What I learned about me

1. The Creator of the Universe considers me.
2. The Heavens hear me.
3. The Earth responds to the God inside of me.

In the beginning of this book I started off telling you four things about our God. 1. **God is Relational** 2. **God is Generational** 3. **He Honors His Word Above All Else** 4. **God is Territorial.** In the remaining chapters we will explore these concepts in detail.

SELAH NOTES

CHAPTER 2
DISCUSSION QUESTIONS

1. Read Isaiah 6. Based on his experience with God, what did Isaiah learn about himself and God? Think about a time God revealed Himself in a real way to you. What did the experience teach you about who God is? What did the experience teach you about yourself?

2. Read the story of the Apostle Paul's conversion experience in Acts 9:1-19. Either in the space provided or in a separate journal recall your own conversion story.

_____
_____
_____
_____
_____
_____
_____
_____
_____
_____
_____
_____
_____
_____
_____
_____
_____
_____
_____
_____
_____
_____

3. Read Acts 9. Paul had a very radical conversion experience. He went directly into ministry soon after. Tell whether or not you believe Jesus became Paul's Lord and Master at the time of his spiritual re-birth.

4. Read John 13. In my testimony I told you that when I received Christ as my Savior He had not yet become my Master. Think about your own story. Are there areas of your life that Christ still needs to be crowned Lord and Master?

5. Read John 14 today. Think about the statement: Salvation is just the foyer. What other rooms of the Lord's House have you had the privilege of exploring?

_____
_____
_____
_____
_____
_____
_____
_____
_____
_____
_____
_____
_____
_____
_____
_____
_____

6. Read Jeremiah 29:11-14. What other rooms in the Master's House would you like to be invited into?

7. Read Matthew 7:7-11, 21:18-22, Luke 11:5-13, John 15:16, Psalms 37. Either in the space provided or in a separate journal write your prayer to the Lord. He is a perfect gentleman who will never take you further than you want to go. Ask Him earnestly to take you past the foyer of His love and into deeper realms within Him.

CHAPTER THREE

GOD IS RELATIONAL

> ✝
>
> **If you want anything extraordinary from God you must become His friend. God gives all the good stuff to His friends.**

If you want anything extraordinary from God, you must become His friend. God gives all the good stuff to His friends. In fact, some of the most influential people in the world God called His friends: Moses, Daniel, David, and Abraham. Look at people throughout history who were able to do mighty exploits for God. If you were to dig around far enough into their histories I believe you'll find a deep and abiding relationship with God. I believe that the famed abolitionist and freedom fighter, Harriet Tubman was a friend of God. She could not have experienced the amazing success she had without being God's friend. I heard a preacher say once, "If we really want to get technical about it, David messed up far more than Saul did." That may very well be true, in our human way of understanding at least. God seemed to have a two-strikes-and-you're-out-of-here-buddy approach with Saul. But here's the thing about Saul—Saul was God's associate. What God and Saul had was purely a business arrangement. David, on the other hand, was God's friend. You and I both know that we will give liberties and allowances to a friend that we would never give to a stranger or even a mere acquaintance. David would not kill Saul out of respect for God and His Word. He understood that even though Saul was broken and demonized he was still God's anointed employee and David wouldn't kill him. But nobody, and I mean *nobody,* could kill David, because David was God's friend. There were times when David would go out to fight, and Israel would be so outnumbered that the whole army would flee. There would be two or three mighty men of valor left fighting beside David, and somehow, someway, David would still win the battle. God fought for David, gave him unprecedented supernatural victories because David was God's friend.

> ✝
>
> **God fought for David and gave him unprecedented supernatural victories because David was God's friend.**

King Solomon, David's son, sinned. The man did everything God told him not to do. Married all those foreign women, brought all those chariots from Egypt. God said because you've sinned I'm going to take the kingdom from you. Nevertheless, I won't do two things. I won't take the whole thing. I'm going to leave you with Judah, because I made a promise to David that one of his ancestor's would always sit on the throne. Also for the sake of your Father David, I won't do this in your lifetime. I'm going to do it in your son's lifetime (1Kings, chapter 11).

> ✝
>
> **Long after you are dead and gone, every God inspired prayer that you ever prayed will remain in the earth.**

David had been dead, buried for many years when God spoke these words to King Solomon, but David was God's friend, and a covenant relationship with God is an eternal inheritance.

Even though David is no longer in the earth, he is still God's friend. God knew it would hurt His friend, to see his son throw away everything that he worked for. God's rebuke of Solomon is a very important passage in scripture, because in this passage, we see a picture of God withholding due judgment out of deference for His friend. Let's face it, David had many military successes, but in the fatherhood department he had failed miserably. Solomon was David's one chance to start again. I think David knew this. As a father he had such high hopes for his son. I believe David prayed many prayers on his child's behalf. I also believe that God hears and honors the prayers of the righteous even from the grave. Long after you are dead and gone from the earth, every God-inspired prayer will remain in the earth. Prayer is mankind's ability to move the hand of God in the heaven and in the earth.

I humbly submit to you today that you can only do that consistently and successfully if you are God's friend. Beloved, if there is one piece of advice that I can give you today it is this: before you leave this planet, make it your top priority to become God's friend.

Heaven and the Relationship Principle

> ✝
>
> **You can have religion and a family legacy in the church but still have no personal relationship with God and therefore have no personal power.**

Not just the Father but all of heaven works on the relationship principle. If you don't believe me just ask the seven sons of Sceva in Acts 19. These boys were the sons of a local high priest and they heard about Paul driving out demons in the name of Jesus.

Let me back up for a moment and say I think this story tells us something very important about deliverance. That's not the focus of our study today, but I believe there's a golden nugget here, so whoever wants it can take it. There are two schools of thought, as it relates to preforming deliverance. Demons are either cast out by the finger of God, or they are punked out. That is to say that God, by divine revelation, puts His finger directly on the problem and the deliverance worker, under the authority of God, casts the unclean spirit out (Luke 11:20).

However, demons can also be cast out by the arm of flesh. That is to say that the deliverance worker exerts their human will over the demon and forces them to come out. 2 Chronicles 32:8 teaches us that the power of God will always bring a better return than the arm of flesh (also see: Psalms 44). The problem with this latter method is that sooner or later, you will meet a demon that is stronger than you. The sons of Sceva were from the Punk-a-Devil-Out-school.

> **I no longer call you servants, because a servant doesn't know his master's business. Now I call you friends.**

They figured if Paul could do it, they could, too. I imagine them saying among themselves, "Heck, if this guy Paul can do it, then we certainly can. After all, our father is the high priest." These boys thought they could ride in on their father's anointing and save the day. See, you can have religion and a family legacy in church but still have no relationship with God, and thus, you have no personal power.

The sons of Sceva would go up to a person who was demon-possessed and they would command the demon to come out. This is how they'd do it. They'd say, "You foul demon spirit I command you in the name of Jesus who Paul preaches to come out of there." Now they must have had a certain measure of success with this method, because the Scriptures say that one day an evil spirit spoke back to them. The demon said, "Jesus I know, and Paul I know, but who are you?" The end result was that that demon mastered them. It beat the brothers so badly that their clothes fell off of them. I realize that many Christians today read that particular story in the Bible and say to themselves, "See there, that's why I don't fool around with the ministry of deliverance. I leave all that casting out of devils to the super holy, and the superhuman Christians." But that's not the moral of the story here. In fact, the moral of the story is just the opposite. The Christian Church was casting out devils in her infancy (see Luke 10:1-23). And these weren't the spiritual elite or the religious scholars of the day either.

These were common lay people who had come into relationship with Jesus. They were successful in their work because they recognized that it was not by their own power, nor by their own might, but by His Spirit that they were able to move in the miraculous (Zechariah 4:6). If the newborn Church had enough moxie and understanding to exercise dominion over fallen angels then certainly the Church, now that she is a teenager, ought to be able to do the same.

The Relationship Principle at Work

The disciples walked with Jesus for three and a half years. They ate with Him and slept in the same dwelling with Him. This was an intimate relationship. Jesus knew all their faults and weakness. It was from this place of intimacy that Jesus elevated them to a place of authority, saying I no longer call you servants, because a servant doesn't know his master's business. Now I call you friends (John 15:15).

And let us not forget about the first man, Adam, who walked and talked with God. God's whole purpose for creating mankind was to have a relationship with thinking, intelligent, rational beings, like Himself. God wants to know your thoughts. Actually, let me say that differently. God wants you to share your thoughts with Him. He wants dialogue—a conversation between two parties. God wants this more than ministry. That's an unconventional concept for most of us to swallow in the church world today, so let me say it again. God wants a relationship with you more than He wants ministry. Go ahead, declare it out loud to yourself:

GOD WANTS A RELATIONSHIP WITH ME MORE THAN HE WANTS MINISTRY

Earlier, in chapter two, I told you that ever since my sixteenth birthday the Lord has given me the most amazing gifts, always on or around my birthday. One year I took myself out to lunch. As I sat in the restaurant, I said to the Lord—quietly inside my head of course—I said, "Well Lord, it's my birthday. What did you get me this year?" The Holy Spirit responded and spoke to my heart right away.

HIM: I have the perfect gift for you this year, but it's nothing like what you think. It's not spiritual.
Me: (confused) What do you mean "not spiritual?"
HIM: This year I'm giving you the gift of balance. Go be a natural person. Get a hobby. Find out who you are and what you like this year.
Me: Seriously, God?
HIM: Seriously.
Me: So no open visions? No visitations?
HIM: Nah, none of that. Go get a hobby.
Me: (silent disapproval)
HIM: I can raise up anyone to preach and teach for me. If I want to, I can raise up a stone to speak for me. But I will never sacrifice you for the sake of the kingdom. Go find Catrina. Find out what she likes and what she doesn't like these days. Go discover what her favorite color is.

God wants an authentic relationship with the real you. I know this study guide is entitled, *Intimacy: The Beginning of Authority*. But I don't want you to focus on the authority part, at least not yet. I want you to take a moment and breathe in the fact that the God of the Universe desires you. Little ole' rejected, unaccepted, you. Do you realize that when God created us, He could have made us to be like machines, never needing to rejuvenate ourselves or to reflect? He'd certainly get the most productivity out of humanity had He made us that way. But He didn't. He chose to make us with the need for something that He Himself doesn't even need: sleep. This says to me that the God of Heaven made us for a greater purpose than our utility. This tells me that we are made for Himself. *Selah*.

SELAH NOTES

CHAPTER 3
DISCUSSION QUESTIONS

1. Read John, chapter 15. Pay special attention to verse 15. Take an honest inventory of your Christian walk. Jesus has called you His friend, but are you a friend to God? What can you do to cultivate a deeper, more intimate friendship with the Lord?

2. Read: Exodus 17:14-16, 1 Samuel, chapters 13 and 15. What fatal flaws do you see in Saul's personality that makes him unsuitable to be used by God?

3. Read 1 Samuel, chapter 16. David's Father didn't seem to think enough of David to present him before the prophet for inspection. Yet God chose David over all his brothers. What does this tell you about God's vision for you versus man's vision for you?

4. Read Acts 19:1-16, Mark 9:38-39, and Mark 16:17. Explain why you think the sons of Sceva were unsuccessful in their attempt at deliverance and why the demons knew Paul's name.

_____
_____
_____
_____
_____
_____
_____
_____
_____
_____
_____
_____
_____
_____
_____
_____
_____
_____
_____
_____
_____
_____

5. Read Matthew 4:1-11 and John 8:44. In the Matthew passage, Satan always starts his sentences with the phrase, "If you are the son of God?" Tell whether you think there is any doubt in Satan's mind whether Jesus is the Christ. What is Satan's motive for using the word if? What do these verses teach us about the tempter and how we should handle temptation?

_____
_____
_____
_____
_____
_____
_____
_____
_____
_____
_____
_____
_____
_____
_____
_____
_____
_____
_____

6. Reflect on the statement: God wants a relationship with you more than He wants ministry. What does a relationship outside of ministry with God look like for you? Would this type of relationship be difficult or easy to foster?

_____
_____
_____
_____
_____
_____
_____
_____
_____
_____
_____
_____
_____
_____
_____
_____
_____
_____
_____
_____

7. Read Psalms 121 and 127. Reflect on why you think a God who never slumbers or sleeps would create humanity with the need to rest.

_____
_____
_____
_____
_____
_____
_____
_____
_____
_____
_____
_____
_____
_____
_____
_____
_____
_____
_____
_____
_____
_____
_____
_____
_____
_____

CHAPTER FOUR

GOD IS GENERATIONAL

> ✝
>
> **When God becomes a friend to your generations He grants what I like to call generational amnesty.**

When God cuts covenant with you He has to cut covenant with everything inside of you, because your lifespan is too short. Scripture says this: a day is like a thousand years to God. We don't have a thousand years. At best, we get 120—and most of us aren't seeing that these days. So to God, a day is like ten human generations—that's assuming each generation gets at least one hundred years. Next to God, your life is like a blade of grass. Your life is too short to fulfill all of God's promises to you. So He has to not only become your friend but a friend to your entire family line, to your future generations. When God becomes a friend to your generations He grants what I like to call **generational amnesty**. The dictionary defines amnesty this way:

Amnesty: 1. a general pardon for offenses, especially political offenses, against a government, often granted before any trial or conviction. **2.** *Law.* an act of forgiveness for past offenses, especially to a class of persons as a whole. **3.** a forgetting or overlooking of any past offense.

> **The word amnesty never represents a single person, but a group of people or governing body. Amnesty is protection and a pardon for an entire people group.**

In other words, you could be guilty as sin. You did it. The smoking gun was in your possession, but a pardon was handed down before the matter even went to court. But here is the thing I want you to understand about amnesty: this word, amnesty, never represents just a single person. It always represents a group. Amnesty is protection, and a pardon for a whole people group.

Amnesty is what Jacob sought the Lord for and received after that whole Dinah debacle in Genesis 34. You remember the story don't you? Dinah is defiled by Shechem, the Hivite prince. Dinah's brothers Levi and Simeon decide to get revenge for her honor. They promise their sister in marriage to the prince on the condition that all the men in the city agree to be circumcised. The Word of God tells us that on the third day, when the men were all sore from the procedure, Simeon and Levi took up their swords and killed all the men in the town.

Jacob is outraged when he finds out what his sons have done. He prays to God, and says, "My sons have done this terrible thing. Now my family line will be wiped from the face of the earth if you don't step in and save me." God does save him. He caused the terror of the Lord to fall upon the people of that area as Jacob and his family left the region in safety.

> **Amnesty is what Rahab got when she hid the spies that Joshua sent out. Jericho burned, but Rahab and everyone related to Rahab was safe.**

Amnesty is what Rahab got when she hid the spies that Joshua sent out (Joshua 2). Jericho burned, just as the spies said, but Rahab and everything and everybody related to Rahab was safe. Rahab's pets were safe. If she had roaches, the roaches were safe and snug inside Rahab's house. That's amnesty.

Paul and Silas were put in jail, because Paul had cast a spirit of divination out of a slave girl that was following them around town (Acts 16:16). Her owners were making a lot of money from her psychic abilities so they raised a claim against Paul, and as a result, the two men were beaten and thrown into prison.

This is demonic backlash and retaliation at its finest. Scripture says that Paul and Silas were praying and singing hymns to God and all the prisoners within were listening to them. At around midnight, all of a sudden, there was a great earthquake that shook the very foundation of the prison. All the prison doors were opened and everyone's bonds became unfastened. I think this passage is supposed to tell us something symbolic about worship.

When the people of God praise Him from a sincere heart, everything and everybody around them can break free.

The jailer thinks to himself, "I can't even begin to explain this to my superiors so I might as well just kill myself." He draws his sword to take his life but Paul tells him, "Wait! Don't do it!" If you believe on the Lord Jesus He'll give you amnesty. You and your whole household will be saved (Acts 16:31).

What I am saying to you, dear reader, is this: if you walk with God and call Him your friend it doesn't matter whether or not the enemy has his hooks in your children right now. God will hunt your children down with His loving kindness and make them His own. He'll find your daughter in the drug house. He'll pursue your grandchildren and your great grandchildren to the ends of the earth. He will do this because He is a God of the generations.

> ✝
> **If you walk with God and call Him your friend, He will hunt your children down with His loving kindness.**
> **He'll find your child in the drug house.**
> **He'll pursue you grandchildren and your great grandchildren to the end of the earth.**
> **He'll do this because He is a God of the generations.**

Heaven and the Generational Principle

The enemy works on this generational principle, too. That's why the Word of God tells us, in at least three places, (Exodus 20:5, Deuteronomy 5:9, Exodus 34:6-7) that the Lord your God is a jealous God who causes the sins of the fathers to be visited upon the third and the fourth generations. This is really important. So important that it's said three times in the Scriptures.

> ✝
> **Too many of us in the body of Christ today are dealing with illegal demonic squatters. We don't understand that when we cut covenant with Christ and certain parameters are met, we are entitled to generational amnesty.**

Notice how the Word doesn't say that the father's sins would be passed down to the children. The word used is visit. You can be visited by a person or a spirit being. So the Scriptures are telling us plainly that these are particular sins that bring about a curse. This particular curse causes demonic visitation and or habitation. That's why the people of God need that generational amnesty that I spoke about earlier. But if you don't know it, you can't have it. The prophet Hosea, speaking through the Spirit of God said: *my people are destroyed because of a lack of knowledge* (Hosea 4:6). We usually quote the first part of the verse, but we neglect the rest of it. The rest of verse 6 says this: *Because you have rejected*

> **✝**
>
> **When you become a Christian, God won't magically slay all your dragons for you, but here's what He will do: when you become a friend to God, He qualifies you to go to war against every bloodline enemy and to recover all.**

knowledge, I also will reject you from being my priest. Since you have forgotten the law I will forget your children.

Translation—no amnesty. God is talking to His leaders in that verse, and He's talking to you and me. What He is saying, is that, yes, my people are destroyed because of lack of knowledge, but it's not because I didn't make all things known to you. It's because you are out of fellowship with Me and with My Word. Then Jesus followed up later and said it like this: the children of darkness are wiser than the children of light (Luke 16:8).

Too many of us in the body of Christ today are dealing with illegal demonic squatters because we don't understand that when we cut covenant with Christ and certain parameters are met, we are entitled to generational amnesty. ***In my father's house there are many mansions. Salvation is just the foyer.*** Here's the thing, when you come to Christ all your problems don't just magically disappear. I've met Christians who say, "I don't need the ministry of deliverance, because when I met Jesus, I left everything at the cross." That, my friends, is a bunch of malarkey. Christians have the same problems that non-Christians have. Our divorce rates, suicide rates, and substance abuse rates are just as high, and in some cases higher than non-Christians. Why is that? How could it be? It's because God doesn't pull out His big pink eraser and blot out all of our problems. That's not His way. Even though

> ✝
> **Your friendship with God qualifies you to go to war on behalf of the bloodline, the people group, the ministry, or the institution you are praying for and to recover all.**

Jesus, through His work on the cross, conquered sin and the grave, we will still have to fight to ascertain complete freedom. *From the days of John the Baptist up until now the Kingdom of God suffers violence. But the violent take it back by force.* (Matthew 11:12)

God won't just magically slay all your dragons for you, but here's what He will do: when you become a friend to God, He qualifies you to go to war against every bloodline enemy and to recover all. David is probably the best example of this. In 1 Samuel, chapter 30, David and his men had just come back from raiding Philistine territory. They returned home to Ziklag and to find that the Amalekites, an old enemy, had raided the city and taken their wives and children into captivity. The reason I say that this is a good example of generational amnesty is because in 1 Samuel, chapter 15:2-3, the Lord, speaking through the prophet Samuel, told Saul, the first king, to go to war with the Amalekites.

I will punish the Amalekites for what they did to Israel when they waylaid them as they came up from Egypt. Now go, attack the Amalekites and totally destroy all that belongs to them. Do not spare them; put to death men and women, children and infants, cattle and sheep, camels and donkeys.

In other words, God was saying, you are to wipe these people completely from the face of the earth. "Don't spare a man, woman, child, camel, or ox, candy bar, or cracker." Okay, so I added the part about the candy bar and the cracker, but you get the gist of it. God commanded them not to take any of their

> **Whatever demons you don't conquer in your generation your children will fight in the next.**

things. The Amalekites and everything they owned were to be devoted to destruction.

Many of us know the story, Saul disobeyed God, and God snatched the kingdom away from him and his family line and gave it to David.

But here's what I really want you to see. Obviously, if David is dealing with the Amalekites fifteen chapters later, Saul had not completely wiped these people from the face of the earth. Beloved, whatever demons you don't route in your generation, your children will fight in the next. That's true in a family, in a people group, in a church, in an institution, in a ministry, or in a nation.

David inquired of the Lord, and asked Him, "Shall I pursue the Amalekites?" God said to Him, "By all means go ahead, pursue." David next asked God, "Will I overtake them?" God told him, "You will surely overtake them, and you will recover everything that has been lost."

Your friendship with God qualifies you to go to war on behalf of that bloodline, people group, ministry, institution, or nation you are praying for and to recover all. *Selah.*

SELAH NOTES

CHAPTER 4
DISCUSSION QUESTIONS

1. Read Genesis 26:1-12 and 28:10-17. What generational blessings do you see at work in this family?

2. Read Genesis 12:10-20 and chapter 27. What generational curses do you see operating in this family?

___

3. Read Genesis, chapters 18-19. God's destroying of the city tells us that apparently, ten righteous people could not be found there. Yet God chose to rescue Lot. Why? What does this act of mercy tell us about His relationship with Abraham? If God showed kindness to Lot because of Abraham, what can you expect that He will do for those whom you love?

4. Who in your family do you need to claim generational amnesty for? Against what?

5. Read Genesis 35:1-15. Three conditions had to be met before God would grant Jacob's family amnesty. In verse 2 Jacob tells his family exactly what those conditions are. Name them and explain the difference between the three.

6. Read Deuteronomy 7:12-16. What are some generational promises God has made to you concerning your family? Or what are some things you would like God to do for your family?

_____
_____
_____
_____
_____
_____
_____
_____
_____
_____
_____
_____
_____
_____
_____
_____
_____
_____
_____
_____
_____
_____
_____

7. Read Deuteronomy 7:1-6. What are the demonic squatters in your personal life that need to be evicted before you can experience the fullness of God? What demonic squatters do you see operating in your family, your community, your church, ministry, and nation?

_____
_____
_____
_____
_____
_____
_____
_____
_____
_____
_____
_____
_____
_____
_____
_____
_____
_____
_____
_____

CHAPTER FIVE

GOD HONORS HIS WORD ABOVE ALL ELSE

> **✝**
>
> **The only thing God is moved by is His Word. So, if I'm going to do business with Him in this realm and in the next, I had better know His Word**

David understood the following about God, and that's why he wrote the 138th Psalms.

I will praise you, O LORD, with all my heart; before the "gods" I will sing your praise. I will bow down toward your holy temple and will praise your name for your love and your faithfulness, for you have exalted above all things your name and your word.

Jesus told the disciples when they questioned Him about the end, "Heaven and earth shall pass away, but my words shall never pass away," (Matthew 24:35). In fact, the very last words written in the Bible is a warning to those who read it. Don't you add or take away from this book. The warning is clear: if you do, you'll lose your eternal inheritance in the kingdom.

Revelation 22:18-19 *I warn everyone who hears the words of the prophecy of this book. If anyone adds to them God will add to him the plagues described in this book. And if anyone takes away from the words of the book* *of this prophecy, God will take away his share in the tree of life and in the holy city, which are described in this book.*

2 Timothy 3:16: *All Scripture is breathed out by God and profitable for teaching, for reproof, for correction, and for training in righteousness.*

We are living in a time and a season when there must be a marriage between the Spirit of God and the Word of God. Oftentimes we meet people in the body of Christ who have an imbalance. They are either full of the Spirit, but they have little or no Word. Or they know the letter of the law, but they have no Spirit. The Word of God tells us plainly that this kind of imbalance is not good, because the letter of the law kills, but the Spirit gives life (2 Cor. 3:6). So what we must press for, what we must contend for, is a union between God's Spirit and His Law. I believe with all my heart that this is what the church must achieve in the coming age. God's people can no longer afford to be imbalanced. I believe God tolerated that when the church was an infant, but now it's time for His people to grow up and for His bride to arise.

The problem with an imbalance is this: you can only prophesy according to your Word level. You can only teach according to your Word level; preachers can only preach, and apostles can only build according to their Word level. That's why the Word of God tells us in 2 Timothy 2:15, *Study to show yourself approved to God, a workman that needs not to be ashamed, rightly dividing the word of truth.*

So, what have you learned so far about the Father? Hopefully, you've learned that you serve a God who is relational, and generational, and who honors His Word above all else. Why is this important to know about Him? Because the only thing God is moved by is His Word. If we are going to do business with Him—in this realm or the next, then we had better know His Word. Because the only thing God responds to is His Word.

> ✝
>
> **Read your Bible. It is the first place God speaks.**

I'll say it again. I can only prophesy according to my Word level. You can only preach or teach according to your Word level. You'll have fluffy preaching if you don't know the Word. Your prayers won't have any bite if you don't pray the Word. They'll go up to the ceiling and fall right back down to the floor. Do you honestly think that the enemy is going to back off because you say so? I'm here to tell you that he won't. Not unless he sees the sword that the writer in Hebrews 4:12 talks about: *Living and active, sharper than any two-edged sword, piercing to the division of soul and of spirit, of joints and of marrow, and discerning the thoughts and intentions of the heart.*

If we understood the magnitude of this aspect of God—that He honors His Word above all else, we would ingest His Word like it's about to go out of print. We would stop depending on other people to tell us who God is, and we would read this marvelous blueprint called the Bible for ourselves. I once heard a preacher tell a congregation, "You don't have to read the whole Bible, that's my job. I'll read it and tell you what it says." Beloved, if you are in a church like that, get up and run away from there as fast as you can. Here's why. I liken that statement to finding out that a very wealthy relative has left you a large sum of money, and the lawyer, or the executor of a will telling you, "You don't have to read the will, there is too much legalese in the document. I'll read it and tell you what it says." You'd tell that lawyer quickly, "No way, buddy! Now, you can help me decipher the legal jargon, but this is my inheritance on the line. Thank you very much, but I'll read it myself." It goes back to the friend thing. Abba is your daddy. You don't need a mediator—a go between—in order to have a relationship with your daddy. He wants to teach you Himself.

> **✝**
>
> **Every Word God ever spoke is still in the earth doing exactly what He told it to do. That's why we still have light. Because He spoke and said, "Let there be light." and there was.**

As for you, the anointing you received from him remains in you, and you do not need anyone to teach you. But as his anointing teaches you about all things and as that anointing is real, not counterfeit—just as it has taught you, remain in him (1 John 2:27).

So what am I saying to you? Am I telling you that you shouldn't go to church? No, I'm saying, read your Bible. If you read your Bible you'll see that the Word of God tells us that the righteous have to assemble together, to encourage one another, so the devil won't make us think we are crazy. What I am also saying is this: you've got a heavenly Father who has left some critical resources on the earth for you. Not only that, but He left a detailed written account of how you can access everything He gave you. Read your Bible. It is the first place God speaks. Earlier in this text, I shared about the first time God ever spoke to me. Let me say this. Everything the Spirit of God said to me could be confirmed in His Word. I was actually raised a Catholic. I told you earlier that I was a voracious reader, so years before I even made a commitment to Christ, I had read most of the Bible through and through. When God spoke to my heart He only validated His Word. After I was saved, all that Word came back to me. His Word can never return back to Him void. It must accomplish what it has been sent forth to do, heal, deliver, and set free. The Word of God is eternal. Every Word God ever spoke is still in the earth doing exactly what He told it to do. That's why we still have light, because in the beginning, God spoke and said, "Let there be light." And there was light. If you really understood the magnitude, the absolute greatness of God's Word, you'd ingest it every way you could. You'd listen to it when you are awake, in the car, in the gym, while you prepare your evening meal. Instead of falling asleep with the television on at night, you'd put the Word on before you go to bed and you'd bathe your subconscious in it while you slept. You'd go to war with it. You'd go to war with it. You'd go to war with it, and you would be victorious.

> ✝
>
> **If we understood the value of the Word of God we would ingest it like it was about to go out of print. We would stop depending on others to tell us who He is, and we would read this marvelous blueprint for ourselves.**

SELAH NOTES

CHAPTER 5
DISCUSSION QUESTIONS

1. Read Ezekiel 3:1-3, Revelation 10:9-10, Psalms 119:103. Tell why you think the Bible often uses the symbolism of eating God's Words. Why is this significant? Explain how the Word of God can be both sweet to the mouth and bitter to the stomach.

2. What strategies are you using to ingest large chunks of God's Word? What is working for you? What can you do better? If you are not currently digesting large chunks of the Word of God, what strategies will you employ so you can begin to do this?

3. Read Ephesians 6. Why do you think the Word of God is included as part of the Christian armor?

4. John 1 gives us a clue as to why God honors the Word so much. According to John what part of the Godhead represents the Word?

5. Read Exodus 4:24-26, Genesis 17:10-14, and Psalms 119:1-4. God tells Moses to go free His people. God then tries to kill Moses along the way, but Zipporah steps in and intercedes on Moses' behalf. What part of God's law did Moses not keep? What do you think God was trying to teach Moses about His nature and His law? What do you learn from this passage about the power of intercession?

6. Read Ezekiel, chapter 37. What do you learn from this passage about the power of the spoken Word of God? How will what you learned inform and change your life?

7. Read Psalms 119. Psalms 119 is the longest chapter in the Bible and in it, the Palmist, most likely David, speaks continually about his love and reverence for God's Word. Highlight the verses in Psalms 119 that especially resonate with you. Why did you choose them?

CHAPTER SIX

GOD IS TERRITORIAL

Psalms 24:1 says: *The earth is the Lord's and the fullness thereof; the world and they that dwell therein.*

David was inspired by the Lord when He wrote this. What is God telling us? He's telling us clearly that He holds all territorial rights to everything on Earth. The Earth is mine, the people who live on it are mine, the cattle, and the grass—all mine. In other words, I'm God and I laugh at anyone who thinks they can lay claim, title, or deed to anything on the earth because everything is mine.

Now, if you are on the Lord's side, and you can stand up under that Word, it'll change your prospective about life. It also becomes a really comforting thought. However, if you aren't on the Lord's side, if you consider yourself to be His enemy, then this is some really

> **If you are on the Lord's side, Psalms 24:1 is a comforting thought. If you aren't on the Lord's side, this is really embarrassing stuff. It's not the kind of information you want getting out.**

embarrassing stuff, and it's not the kind of information you want to get out to the public at large. John 1 says it like this:

In the beginning was the Word, and the Word was with God, and the Word was God. He was with God in the beginning. Through him all things were made; without him nothing was made that has been made.

Colossians 1:15-16 takes it one step further and says it like this— talking about Jesus:

He is the image of the invisible God. The firstborn of all creation. For by him all things were created, in heaven and on earth, visible and invisible, whether they be: thrones or dominions or rulers, or authorities, all things where created through him and for him. And he is before all things and in him all things hold together.

When the writer uses words like: thrones, dominions, rulers, authorities, he's talking about angelic forces—both good and evil. Like Paul does in Ephesians 6, the writer is giving you a breakdown of the demonic kingdoms. And he says they all were created for Jesus and that they work for Him. I submit before you today that another word for territory is authority. God owns all territory thus He has all authority. Everybody, including Satan, works for God.

> ✝
>
> **Another word for territory is authority. God owns all territory, thus He has all authority. Everybody, including Satan, works for God.**

You remember King Ahab, Jezebel's husband? God said this man was the most wicked king in the history of both Israel and Judah put together. The prophet Micaiah tells us that one day God called a meeting in heaven and all the angelic beings came. This is actually in the Word of God (you can read about it in 1 Kings, chapter 22 for yourself). Micaiah says that the host of heaven were standing before God on His right and His left. Hum, on His right and on His left? Now, where else have we heard this phraseology before? Matthew 25:31-46:

When the Son of Man comes in his glory, and all the angels with him, he will sit on his glorious throne. All the nations will be gathered before him, and he will separate the people one from another as a shepherd separates the sheep from the goats. **He will put the sheep on his right and the goats on his left.**

> ✝
>
> Not only does God own all territory, He likes to give some of it away. He really likes to give territory to His friends. He gave Adam the garden, He gave Abraham Canaan and He gave Moses the children of Israel.

Micaiah says he sees the angels all around the throne of God but there is a distinction between the two groups, some are on His right-hand side, and some are on His left. Just like the picture Jesus draws for us with the sheep—those that follow the shepherd—and the goats—those that want to go their own way and do their own thing. Micaiah says that God asks a question to all those assembled before Him. "Who shall entice Ahab to go to war so that he can die in battle?"

Micaiah says a few of the angelic beings were discussing the matter, throwing some ideas around, when a lying spirit steps forth. The lying spirit says, "I'll do it by becoming a lie in the mouths of his prophets." God says alright, get to it. You will have success.

Then of course there is Saul. After the Lord rejected him, He sent an evil spirit to torment him. Scripture tells us clearly that this evil spirit was sent to Saul not from Satan but from God (1 Samuel 16).

God can command a rebel spirit to torment a man because everyone works for God. God can call a meeting in the heavenly realms and those that hate and utterly despise Him, show up, because EVERYONE works for God. Think about it. If the big boss on your job calls a mandatory meeting what other choice do you have, but to show? Well so it is in the spirit realm. Satan is the king over the demonic realm, but Jehovah is the King of Kings and the Lord of Lords. He is the boss of all bosses.

All things are made for Him and by Him, be they thrones, rulers, or principalities. If you understand this, this will shift how you see yourself, how you see the earth, and how you see demons. Everything was made for and by God. *Selah.*

Not only does God own all territory, but He likes to portion some of it out. He gives territory to everybody, but He really likes to give territory to His friends. He gave Adam the garden, He gave Abraham Cannan, and He gave Moses the children of Israel. God will either give out literal territory or figurative territory.

Literal territory: God will give you a house.

Figurative territory: God will give you a child.

In fact, God has given every person on the planet territory. And He expects us to do with it the same thing He told Adam to do with the garden: cultivate it, subdue it, and protect it.

When the Lord first began to speak to me about this concept of territory, He told me that He has given every person on the planet territory.

He explained that territory is a part of our inheritance as children of God. Whether we choose Him or not, whether we accept Him or not. Territory is a "gift." It took me a minute to wrap my head around that idea because so often we think that God only gives gifts to us chosen Christian people. But try this concept on for size. If you were to trace Jesus' ancestry you'd find that every people group on the planet has a genetic stake in Jesus Christ. Isn't that beautiful?

> God has given every person on the planet territory. He expects us to do with it the same thing He told Adam to do with the garden: cultivate it, subdue it, and protect it.

God gives territory to all His children. As I said, I had a hard time wrapping my mind around this concept of God giving territory to everybody, so He broke it down to me like this:

HIM: If a drug addict would pray over her children before they left the house for school in the morning, I would hear her prayer and honor her request.
Me: (stunned) A crackhead, really?

HIM: Of course. Her children are the only thing she has left. Everything else now belongs to the pipe. But those children are still her territory.

God will hear your prayers concerning your territory. Again, Saul, the first king of Israel, is an excellent example of this. Even after the Lord rejected Saul as king, when Saul went up to battle, if it was a part of the territory that Saul was supposed to take, God gave him victory. Often enough I've spoken to intercessors who are beginning to grow in the things of God—and like always—the more we grow the more we see. I've watched these same intercessors become frantic when God opens their eyes and they began to see the true spiritual condition of their prayer target. "God is showing me Perversion, and Witchcraft in my territory, oh no! What in the world am I going to do?" They become like Dorothy in the The *Wizard of Oz* saying, "Lions, tigers, and bears, oh my!"

I certainly don't mean to make light of their distress, because seeing things as they truly are in the spirit realm can sometimes be a very unsettling thing. However, these intercessors act as if the devils in question just arrived by car or by boat. The reality is they've been there all along. You just couldn't see them. But here's the good news: God never shows you anything you are not prepared to deal with. And if He's showing it to you, that means He intends to equip you and to teach you how to route it.

---

†

God never shows you what He won't prepare you to deal with. If He's showing it to you, that means He intends to equip you, to teach you how to rout it.

HEAVEN & THE TERRITORY PRINCIPLE

Two stories in particular teach us that all of Heaven works on the Territory Principle: Jude 1:9, and the story of the demon-possessed man who lived near the tombs in Luke 8. Jude 1:9 says:

But even the archangel Michael, when he was disputing with the devil about the body of Moses, did not dare to bring a slanderous accusation against him, but said, "The Lord rebuke you!"

> ✝
>
> The archangel Michael never stepped outside of his boundaries when confronting Satan. He overcame him by calling on the highest authority of all.

The writer of Jude tells us that there was a dispute over Moses' body between the archangel Michael and Satan. Michael, although he is an archangel did not step outside of the boundaries of his territory. Michael didn't tell Satan, "Get away from these bones! You don't have the right to touch them." He didn't do this because Michael understands territory. Michael knows the same thing that Satan would whisper to Jesus as he showed Him all the kingdoms of the world in the blink of an eye. That all authority on earth had (before Jesus's death and resurrection) been given to Satan.

> **✝**
>
> **Some demonic structures have been put in place for God's redemptive work. That's why intercessors should exercise care when attempting to tear these structures down. Authority in the Spirit realm is regulated to the boundary lines of your coast.**

Michael dealt with him by saying, "Satan, the Lord rebukes you."

Michael overcame Satan not by getting into a test of wills with him, but by calling on the greatest authority of all. The one who owns all authority. Jesus' handling of the demons in Luke 8 also shows that all of heaven works on this territory principle:

They sailed to the region of the Gerasenes, which is across the lake from Galilee. When Jesus stepped ashore, he was met by a demon-possessed man from the town. For a long time this man had not worn clothes or lived in a house, but had lived in the tombs. When he saw Jesus, he cried out and fell at his feet, shouting at the top of his voice, "What do you want with me, Jesus, Son of the Most High God? I beg you, don't torture me!" For Jesus had commanded the evil spirit to come out of the man. Many times it had seized him, and though he was chained hand and foot and kept under guard, he had broken his chains and had been driven by the demon into solitary places. Jesus asked him, "What is your name?" "Legion," he replied, because many demons had gone into him. And they begged him repeatedly not to order them to go into the abyss. A large herd of pigs was feeding there on the hillside. The demons begged Jesus to let them go into them, and he gave them permission. When the demons came out of the man, they went into the pigs, and the herd rushed down the steep bank into the lake and was drowned.

The demons asked Jesus if he would send them into the pigs. What they were really saying was, "Please Jesus, can we stay in this area. Pretty please!" Jesus honored the demons' request. He did not send them to the abyss but into the pigs as they requested. In order to fully understand what Jesus did in this story, we have to understand that some things—including demonic structures—have been put in place for God's redemptive purposes. That's why intercessors should never just run around town willy-nilly, pulling down things in the Spirit realm. Your authority in the spirit realm is regulated by the boundary lines of your territory. Since Jesus, being God, owns all territory, He could tell the demons to go or stay as He desired. We can probably guess why the demons wanted to stay in the region. They were on assignment. They did not want to go to the abyss, and they certainly didn't want to have to report back to their superiors and say they had failed to secure their region. The next best option was to be sent into the pigs. I believe that Jesus did not send the demons to the abyss because He had plans to use them to further His work of salvation in that area.

> **Every force in the spirit realm must respond to the individual who puts a demand on their territory.**

He is the image of the invisible God. The firstborn of all creation. For by him all things were created, in heaven and on earth, visible and invisible, whether they be: thrones or dominions or rulers, or authorities, all things where created through him and for him. And he is before all things and in him all things hold together (1Colossians 1:15-17).

Translation: Everybody works for God.

The Territory Principle at Work

I recently had the privilege of counseling a young lady who came to me about her husband's unbelief. Her husband has an illness which he has struggled with for many years. The illness severely affects him and has defined their entire married lives. One day, in a dream, the Lord showed the wife the illness. She saw it crawl out of her husband's body. She saw what a hideous monster this particular affliction was. She also saw that the disease was not the big, bad wolf that it had magnified itself to be. It was actually deformed and crippled. She woke up from the dream knowing that if her husband would rebuke it, it would come out at once. But, it had been with him most of his life, and although she had received revelation in the dream, her husband had not. The husband believed that he was powerless to deal with this particular devil.

I listened intently to her story, and afterward asked her this question, "So what are you prepared to do?"

"There's not really much I can do, until my husband stands up and takes authority over this thing."

"On the contrary," I said. "I think we may be able to find a loophole in the Scriptures. What does the Word of God say about a married person's body? It's not theirs, it belongs to their spouse. When the two marry they become one."

God gave her the dream because her husband's body is her territory. Now she has the knowledge with which she can go to war, and as she stands on the Word of God she will be victorious. On a personal note, I have been in healing services, ministered, laid hands on the sick, felt the healing virtue of God go out of me, and watched people recover. Then there have been times when I've gotten home and couldn't even rebuke a tiny headache. I would say, "God, what's going on here, what the heck is this?" In those times God would give me a different strategy.

"Ask your husband to pray for you," the Spirit would say.

So, I'd say, "Wesley, I've had this headache all day, I've been rebuking the enemy, but it's still here." We'd be in bed for the night and my husband could be half asleep but when he would reach over in the darkness and lay his hand on my head, it would leave instantly. That's territory, and every force in the spirit realm must respond to the individual who puts a demand on their territory.

SELAH NOTES

CHAPTER 6
DISCUSSION QUESTIONS

1. Read Genesis 1. What literal territory has God given you? Now that you understand the concept of territory, how will you subdue, cultivate, and, protect this territory?

2. Read Genesis 17. What figurative territory has God given you? Now that you understand the concept of territory, how will you subdue, cultivate, and, protect this territory.

___
___
___
___
___
___
___
___
___
___
___
___
___
___
___
___
___
___
___
___
___
___

3. Read Jeremiah 33:3, John 16:13, and Psalms 32:8-9. Ask God to speak to you regarding your territory. Write down any impressions He places on your heart in the space provided below.

_____

_____

_____

_____

_____

_____

_____

_____

_____

_____

_____

_____

_____

_____

_____

_____

_____

4. Read Genesis 18:17-19. Explain why you think the God of the whole earth cares whether Abraham knows about His plans.

5. Read Numbers 35. In order to maintain protection from the blood avenger, the manslayer—who had been found not guilty of intentional homicide—had to remain in the city of refuge until the death of the high priest. Drawing upon what you have learned about territory, explain why.

6. Read Mark 5:1-20. In chapter 6, I talked about Jesus allowing the demons to stay in the region to fulfill His redemptive purposes in that area. Give your thoughts on what those redemptive purposes might be.

7. Read Matthew 8:28-29, Mark 1:21-28, and James 2:19. What truths do these passages reveal to you about the nature of both God and demons?

CHAPTER SEVEN

INTIMACY THE BEGINNING OF AUTHORITY

So this is how this journey to authority begins. You walk up to the altar one Sunday, and you give your life to Christ. You become a citizen of His kingdom, and you start to learn about the Creator and His awesome love for you. One day you muster up the courage, take a leap of faith, and you start a conversation with Him. On another day, you take one more courageous step toward Him, and you dare to listen, to hear Him speak back to you. Now you've done it, the thing that 99% of the earth's population will never do: you've entered into dialogue with the Living God. The King of Kings begins to visit you and tell you what you mean to Him. One day you find yourself believing it. One day in the ultimate act of courage, you open the door to your heart and you invite Him in to shine His light of truth upon your life. Now you see for the first time in a long time your garden, your territory. The thing He gave you to cultivate and protect. It's an absolute mess.

Jesus is looking around your garden, and you wished you'd done better. Wished you'd taken the time to spruce up the place a bit. You can't meet His gaze for fear of seeing His disappointment with you. When out of the corner of your eye, you see a slight motion. The Creator of the Universe is stooping down. He's surveying the ground beneath His feet. With His finger, He's writing something in the dirt.

"An enemy has done this," He says. "See, he climbed in through that window over there, trampled through your garden and set fire to your walls."

He is angry, and you know it. You can tell by the deep, low reverberating timbre of His voice. It scares you, shakes everything inside of you. You know now why they call Him the Lion of Judah. You stand there wringing your hands, shifting uncomfortably from one foot to the next, still unable to meet His gaze. But then He calls you by name, and He smiles the same smile that won your heart on that first day. He's not writing in the dirt anymore. He's standing upright, reaching out His hand to you. That's when you realize, He's not angry with you at all. His anger is directed at the one who took your stuff. The enemy who climbed in through your window, trampled through you garden, and burned your walls.

"You know what I think?" He says, His voice becoming smooth, and gentle again.

You shake your head no. He's God, how could you even possibly begin to conceive His thoughts?

"I think that now is the time to recover all. Let's go get your stuff back."

He's right here now, beloved, and He's holding out His hand to you. Now is the time to recover all. Now is the time to get everything back.

SELAH NOTES

EPILOGUE

AN INVITATION TO JOIN THE FAMILY OF GOD

If you've never made a commitment to Jesus, I invite you now to make Him the Savior of your life. Salvation is ultimately where this journey begins. If you would like the Lord Jesus to come and live in your heart simply pray the following prayer:

Lord Jesus,

I believe you and I believe in you. I believe you are the Word made flesh who came to live among humans. I believe that not only are you the son of the Living God, you are the only God. I acknowledge that the only way to eternal life for me is through you. I believe that you came to earth, lived and died as a man to save me from the penalty of sin and death. So Lord I receive your perfect gift of salvation. I receive you as my Savior, I ask that you come into my heart and become my friend, my Master and My Lord. Live inside of me forever more. In your name Jesus I pray. Amen.

Beloved, if you prayed that prayer you've just been born again. Right now the angels in heaven are rejoicing over you. You see, they understand something that I pray you understand too—if no one else ever on the planet would have accepted the gift of salvation Jesus would have still shed his divinity, come to the earth as a man, lived for thirty-three and a half years, and died—just for you. Welcome to the kingdom. Salvation is the foyer. Enter in to so much more.

ABOUT THE AUTHOR

Catrina J. Sparkman is a licensed, ordained minister and the founder of The Ironer's Press Ministries, which hosts Prayer Parties—a seasonal gathering of intercessors from all over the Midwest, as well as The Fourth Watch—a 3-6am prayer meeting, that happens every Friday morning in her home city. She is the author of *Doing Business with God: An Everyday Guide to Prayer and Journaling*.

An inspirational speaker, consultant, presenter, and personal empowerment coach for various churches and ministry organizations, Catrina teaches on prayer, the prophetic ministry, and healing. She lives in Madison, Wisconsin, with her husband, Wesley, and their three beautiful children. She can be reached at doingbusinesswithgod@gmail.com.

BOOKING INFO:

To book Minster Sparkman for your next ministry event please contact: Kubernesis Administrative Services on behalf of the Ironer's Press. T: 858 663.7810 kubernesis.info@gmail.com

www.ingramcontent.com/pod-product-compliance
Lightning Source LLC
Chambersburg PA
CBHW020143130526
44591CB00030B/183